Untreated:

A Crucial Note-to-Self

Raw Words for a Complex Time

Untreated by John Abraham Reynolds

Minneapolis, MN

© 2019 John Abraham Reynolds. All right reserved.

ISBN: 978-1-7336345-3-3

Dear Admired,

I invite you to the first.

Please know that I wrote this book because it was necessary.

This book is not trying to be anything. It's not trying to fit in anywhere, or appeal to a certain group. It's not fiction. It's not classical poetry. It's not an essay, or scientific psychiatry.

It's simply a note-to-self.

It's an attempt to **find** and **restore** the **Autonomous Individual** in each and every one of us. It's also an attempt to locate and outline the **Powerful Psychic Entity** that has been created by Social Media.
These words are nothing more than an attempt to shine light on what is furthest from the mind and closest to the heart.

As you read, I hope you see that this book hints towards a way of living. It hints at a way of looking at issues, relationships, and decisions in Life with a clearer scope. It's really a fusion of opposites. It's an age-old foundation draped in contemporary cloth.

Sometimes in this Life, when two opposite things meet and find a space where both can exist in harmony, magic happens.
That's what the Individual is.
The Individual is magic. The Individual is the ability to remain calm when tragedy strikes. It's the ability to move through your problems with grace. It's the ability to be flexible when others are rigid. It's the ability

to see when others are blind. It's the ability to get up when your opponent thinks he has you beat. It's the ability to remain stable in Life through the power of being limber.

I hope that most of these messages are intrinsic. I hope that some of these messages you know but have not yet realized.

In an era where reality is more distorted than ever, it's important for us to *look up* every once and awhile.
To look up at the scene around us, to look up to the people around us, and most importantly, to look in to see who we

really are. Because that's where the magic is. That's where Life is.
That's where the meaning is hiding.

By no means is this an ending. It's just a step in a certain direction. The blank space in this book is intentional. I left it for you. I left it for your own thoughts, your own writing, and your own vision.

With love,

John Abraham Reynolds

One

We exist not yet in triumph my friends. Due to the inherent power of the Collective Intellect that resides within each one of us, it has become all but necessary for the Modern Spiritual Being to spend time with an atheist point of view. For time spent in this place ensures two things:

1.   That One is able to locate, contact, and utilize The Intellect to its most optimal degree.

2.   And with that, One is able to experience the subtle liberating relationship that exists between The Spirit and The Intellect, therefore extinguishing the valid contempt that currently lives between the two, thus giving way to a *Harmonious Life*. God Bless.

Birth

In more ways than not

it is our ever-present duty

to stand in-between

The Infinite Unknown of the Universe

and

The Finite Known

we call Reality.

If we can do this,

we will be in position

to bring that which resides in

The Infinite Unknown

into reality,

and give it Life.

That is Adventure.

And Adventure is Reality's gift to all.

Death

There is no reason to be afraid of feeling trapped in darkness when the body dies.

You are no longer in it.
It's as simple as that.

It is a natural thing for us to envision death in this state.
For this vision is inherent with the burden of consciousness.

The key is to realize it as something of our nature,
and then to see it as nothing more than a contrived illusion.

It's a futile exercise in Self-sabotage to subject your Soul to the human crafted condition of *eternal claustrophobia*.
For it is indeed a condition of the human Mind.

Once the human body dies
the Soul leaves...
And the Soul is many, many things...

But human is not one of them.

Feelectric

And so then I suppose it's appropriate
to ask why we are all aiming at a Life of eternal,
uninterrupted happiness?
We know that this state is not possible,
because for happiness to exist,
it requires its opposite - whatever that may be.

And it's in this light that true vision appears,
letting us know that happiness isn't the goal,
but the byproduct of remaining true to yourSelf. No matter what.

I Live for You

The Ego's initial reaction

to the realization of The Spirit

is usually one of repulsion,

for contained in The Spirit's arrival

is the very thing The Ego fears most:

Vulnerability.

"A Soliloquy" by: Rake

If I don't take control, someone else will. If I don't bare my soul for those to see, then someone else will burn it up for a fee.

But then again we live in the age of information...where one second you could read an article that tells you we are all that's left, and then read an article that tells you that you are all that's right...and seriously...hasn't anyone tried to look IN? I wish I could be a Hero...that's all I ever wanted... but maybe you can...maybe if you listen, the answer will arrive...right now it seems like everything is going to hell, and well, that might just be the dEVILS's spell...and if I listen to you, then it might be true, that all I am waiting on is a clue...but what if that clue is gone, or hidden in a song? There are camps that tell you that kind of cognition is healthy, while others will numb you to make them appear wealthy...

But then again, who knows? Ain't that just how the story goes? One right, one wrong, put them together and you got a song...but one clue, plus me and you,
well that's an all night
RENDEZVOUS.
I think I hate myself because I ain't myself...All I want is a dollar...that's it...for if I have a dollar, then I will still have my Dream...it's only when I make

enough to buy the extra-cream that I develop low-self esteem.

Just My Imagination

In the truest sense

of the word,

HUMAN *is*

struggle and personal battle.

On this level,

we're all the same.

We are One.

It's only when we being

to cloth these

elements in modern dress that we become

unique.

Pneumerals

Anytime we add numbers to a situation,

we swing our front-door wide open and

invite Anxiety to

come rushing in.

This form of Anxiety, at its base, is a

product of our supreme knowledge.

It's true that

we know what a "3" feels like standing next

to a "10"

and

we know what a "300" feels like standing

next to a "1000."

I'm not calling this a bad thing,

for it certainly has its place. All I am

trying to do is outline the relationship,

hopefully granting you the ability to

IGNORE

This Anxiety when it enters your home without necessity.

The Rub

SUBCONSCIOUS APPEAL = INVOLUNTARY ACTION

To ignore the power of the Subconscious is
all Fun and Games
until the Subconscious starts dictating the
"Fun and Games" to cater to its own needs.
And when we remain blind of this power,
the chaos within the Mind boils towards
the surface of the skin.
And the skin eventually gives way,
allowing the chaos that was once in the
mind to morph into Action.
And that's when
Evil happens for Evil's sake.

Gas

If this experience were an automobile,

the Ego would be the gas,

while the Spirit is the car itSelf.

You are the driver.

You need both to live and thrive

in this world,

but without the automobile,

the gas is nothing but combustible liquid

on the pavement,

simply waiting to cause disaster.

It's a balancing act,

Driver.

Drive your car.

It's ok to let it drive itSelf sometimes,

but never put your faith in the gas.

It's only purpose is to explode.

Stay

In this Life,

you can fight to

surrender

or

you can fight to

keep your stay.

To fight to

surrender

is to discover the truth

and to fight to stay

is to live life in the elevator.

To surrender is

to destroy limits

and to stay is to keep building more.

And if you ask me,

the staying is the chore.

Note It Friend, Note It

Your Talent is what is accessed when the heart is liberated and Rational Critique is thrown out of a top-story window and run over by a large van upon impact...

That's when your talent is on full display and the Spirit arrives on Earth, ready to dance...

but, like every single other thing on this Earth...

any positive force must be met by its negative match...

and when one follows the course mapped above...

The Spirit is met by extreme burden and responsibility...

If the Spirit is liberated...

it is up to the Mind to mediate...

to keep The Spirit's force in check...

By all means let it go... but if it gets to

a place where grand harm is desired...

recognize it and adjust...

the Positive is met by the Negative...

and when the Spirit is brought to live on

this Earth...

The Devil comes with it...

The Real World

Perhaps

the chatter in our minds won't quit

because we're afraid

of what will appear if we stop talking.

What I Thought Was

It's always in the dark-hours

of the night...

Those elusive pre-dawn moments...

That the world becomes still enough for

yourSelf to speak out...

And yourSelf is strong.

And yourSelf is true.

And it's in this voice that you will

find the entity that will always be there

for you.

Through and Through.

Self Respect

Self Respect is of the highest wisdom.

But to respect the Self,

one must know the Self.

And to know yourSelf

in a world where everyone is trying

to tell you who you are is

a tall task.

Unison

In order to dance

    in the sun and have fun,

you must also sit

    in the rain and feel pain.

For it's between the two

that you will find You.

    And after all,

that's what you're here to do.

The Lip

The closer your external experience gets to Death,

the harder the Conscious Mind is going to try to hold on.

This relationship is a product of the senses,

which have been fine tuned for the world we live in,

thus giving it reason to be here.

But let it be known,

that contained in this relationship is also the potential for our biggest fall,

which is not becoming our Self.

Providence

Upon the realization

of the many false barriers

we set for ourSelves

rises the great sensation

of Potential.

And it's in Potential

that we find Life

and it's in Life

that we find meaning

and it's in meaning

that we find our Self.

St. Johnny

We must remain active

as both

The Teacher

and

The Student.

For in this experience,

it's the only way to

stay Prudent.

The April Sun

The purpose of Beauty is to let us know

that something special is happening

at a single moment in Time,

so we can experience it before it ends.

For once Beauty is done,

it's gone forever...

That's why Love exists.

Because

Love knows no limits,

and doesn't respond to Time.

Love is unique,

and gives Life its Internal Rhyme.

For Love looks forward,

towards the next mountain to climb,

and has the chance to Live Forever,

between Your Heart and Mine.

Suppose to do

It's ok to

KNOW that

you CAN

do something.

Deep Respect

If you really ask yourSelf what it took for you to get to where you are RIGHT NOW, what you'll see is a vast landscape of all those who came before you.

You'll see their work.
You'll see their sacrifices.

And it's in this vision
that gratitude comes rushing in.
And when gratitude collides with Life,
Hate is forced to collide with the Knife.

Just how far was the walk

If you can feel the fire,

and you are sure you didn't start it,

go with it,

let it burn,

and allow it to live with you.

What will follow

is what was meant to be.

The bad will burn

and the good will ignite.

Once the fire goes out,

pick up the ashes

to uncover the trophy.

Then proceed to give thanks.

For what was once hidden

is now seen,

and the dawn is given permission to start

the fire once again.

Please Rise

If hate exists in the Mind,

it poisons the body

until extradited.

You can live with hate for a long time,

of that we are sure.

But to die with hate is what we should fear,

for in a way it leaves something undone,

and anything undone has potential to create regret,

and dying with regret is something we strive our entire Life to prevent.

Dear You

This experience isn't all good...

It takes a lot of sacrifice...

and that can be hard on the Ego...

really hard...

Outlining the Ego is one of the most

difficult things a human can do...

and in any case, complete destruction of

the Ego is not desirable...

For the Ego is the entity that allows us to

feel like individuals...

and that is vital to function in this

world...

However,

in order for you to know that you have an

Ego and are indeed an individual...

you must be able to identify its polar

opposite...

which is complete oneness with the

universe...

Tire

When basking in the light of

The Cycle of Life,

the only thing illuminated is the

Present Moment.

Will Be Televised

If the very notion of a Broader Mind

is still out there,

then in what frame of Mind is it

warranted to stop pushing forward?

And if it's ok to stop,

what else is left to do?

That's the great power of stagnation.

And if we aren't careful,

that power will define us.

Tea and Coffee

He was ordinary,

She was strange.

The two met and things

were set to change.

As she got closer,

he got further away.

As he got further away,

she started to give way.

For if the two had never met,

she'd never be strange

and he'd never be ordinary.

And we'd all be lost,

in what we are.

For what we are is only possible

if what we aren't is present.

And in that,

we can see how crucial the Individual is

in the face of the group.

It starts in You.

Your Hero

Let me tell you a story about the greatest hero I ever knew.

I knew a guy,

and this guy needed help.

He looked left,

He look right,

but the help wasn't in sight.

He looked up,

He looked down,

and he was left with a frown.

The outside world was out to get him,

and not a Soul wanted to be his synonym.

For this man was bitter,

and this man was dry.

Everyone was against him,

No matter how hard he tried.

Until one day this man looked in,

and it was there that he found his

Original Sin.

He found that what he needed wasn't in the world,

but in his heart.

He uncovered what he already knew,

and stopped searching for what

he'd never find.

The greatest hero of your story is **you**.

And no matter what happens on the outside,

the Hero remains within,

and it's

always ready to help you win.

Return to-

Due to the mass extinction of the Individual's Soul,

we've been abandoned to attribute the terrifying workings of the Collective Unconscious

to the workings of our Self.

This pathology leaves no room for meaningful Alchemy.

It forces the Inner Being to take a form opposite of

its original purpose of Total Refuge.

This generates a feeling of ever lasting entrapment.

And that creates

a claustrophobic existence generated by
One's own thoughts.

And when the only avenue to emancipation
from this horrific state remains to be in
the very genesis of its existence,
It's usually the last place we look for the
answer.

Last

Know that if you knock,

The door shall be answered.

Which means when you need it,

it will be there.

That's faith in its purest form.

And faith in the face of fear

is the only way to be

who You *can* be.

Tumbling on a BigTime Mattress

Entitlement is a thing to be wary of.

It often runs unseen,

hidden from the Conscious Mind,

and wreaking havoc on the value to be found.

For value exists in things that aren't given,

and to obtain anything that isn't given,

one must commit to grueling, dedicated work.

In this Light,

work isn't the enemy, but the savior.

The trick is to find the medium that allows *work* to deliver value.

And that trick,

is in your heart.

It somehow already knows.

73118

The Spirit opposes apathy at all costs,

allowing Life to be the translator

of your commitment,

and to illustrate what you do when the

going gets tough.

Nothing Greater Here

In THIS WORLD,

Taking measures of extreme safety and

security

force us into a state of

BLIND IGNORANCE.

Our destination is known,

and it isn't tragic.

What is tragic is acting like we can

prevent it,

and doing so at the expense of chasing our

goals

and fulfilling our dreams.

All of that is an act of buying into

The Safety that is sold to us as

The Answer to

The Fear that is injected into us.

And

That's lethal.

Look behind to find The Truth.

Man, Virtue Dr.

One of the most virtuous of all Human
Traits is
Adaption.
And in Adaption, is Patience.

We never know what we're going to need,
and in that,
it's known that it's a difficult thing to
prepare.

Bulletproof Preparation is required to stay
true to oneSelf,
and it requires great patience and keen
adaption.

What's true to oneSelf is what is needed by
The World,

so sit tight.

Your time is on the horizon.

Dielogue

Practice the Art of Dying

to access the Art of Living.

It's true that Life could not exist

with Death.

So stashing Death

into the depths of the Mind does

nothing but disrupt the Conscious Harmony

that is required for true,

Inner-Peace.

The sooner we understand this,

the sooner Peace will arrive.

And when Peace is found,

all of THIS becomes a lot simpler.

But this is no simple task,

and that's what makes it an Art.

Betcha' Buy Gold

The Body is an instrument designed for

The Mind to perceive this world, and

The Mind is an instrument designed to

translate

the perceptions into a Voice called The

Ego.

The other Voice,

the one that runs along with Intuition,

has evidence of being

designed by the Spirit.

And because this Voice is the

ever-critiquing nature of The Ego,

it's clear to see that it's not of This

World at all,

but rather of something we can feel,

yet can't understand completely.

Paradox

Hidden in the ability to not care about

that of which is outside of your control,

is the aspect of

pure, concentrated, undiluted

Self-Autonomy.

And in this experience,

in This Life,

when something is outlined and crystalized

to the point where it seems like nothing

stands behind it,

we can know for certain

that we have found the Source,

and the Source of ultimate Self-Control is

Self-Recognition in the face of

YouR SELF CRAFTED ILLUSION.

TwoParadox

The sooner we sacrifice out attachment

to our Individual for the greater good

of the family,

    the community,

and

        the world,

The sooner we'll recognize the power

invested

in our own Individual to Change.

And when it comes to that of which a Single

Person can do,

I see no greater power

than the power to change.

With the Angels

Dear Me,

If there are any holes in the shield that is indeed provided by Slice of Divine within your Soul,

it will,

at all costs,

expose You to It.

It will work its way through the reality we are living in,

communicate in the medium available on this earth,

and expose You,

*to **You**.*

If you fail to answer this call,

you will forever look

*to place your faith in external sources.
Eternally looking for an external place of
Refuge within the Chaos.*

*Maybe the external source is
an ideology, or a leader,
or worst of all,
a system of belief that you're sold.
And
when you rely on an external source for
pure salvation of
the Soul,
you will play into that game that is
created for you,
and miss the opportunity to create the game
for yourSelf.*

4Every1

Negativity is rooted

in the Self witnessing

altered versions of its Self,

yet,

refusing to accept them as possible,

thus,

searching for another avenue to release

the very energy that is gained

in realizing ultimate Oneness with the

Universe.

Keep Safe

The longer you hold on to the handle

that is keeping you attached to the

illusion of

Ultimate Control,

The longer you will be

A Victim of the

False Freedom

that is created by mishandling the great

gift of

Free-Will.

For invested in Free-Will is the

unmeasurable power

to both create and destroy

your own Life.

To identify this is the first step

towards freeing the Self.

Clee-shay

Ideas that are simple to understand

are only simple because they

have been around a long time.

And

The only way an idea can stand the test of time

is to remain Universally true across the dimensions.

By way of that,

we see that it's the simple things that are

the most difficult to implement,

yet remain the most potent to inflict

change.

Bound Together

The only way

to stay

ready to die

is to

spend your days

doing what allows

you to live.

Free-Verse?

I write in free-verse

for Us.

I do it so you can be sure

that what ends up appearing on the page

remains the closest and most authentic

version of the sounds I was hearing

at the time of each

delivery.

The Cross

I have found that true inspiration in this world

comes from working against all that is feared

by the Conscious Mind.

It's found on a Journey that

ignores the pitfalls of rational reason

and keeps away from rotting in The Underground.

It's in this very idea,

and in this very way,

that we start to see how something as

elusive as Art

can be so meaningful.

For if Reason and Logic lie in one-hand,

Inspiration and Art lie in the other,

and between them is Harmony.

And as far as I can tell,

Harmony itSelf

is where we are meant to be.

12/XX/99

In the same way our Ancestors were

tasked with separating the Self from

the Ego in order to gain autonomy,

We are tasked with separating the Self from

the Feed.

It's crucial to realize that

the Feed isn't merely entertainment,

but an Active Voice that

makes its Home in all of our Minds.

It's alive.

The Recipe for Disaster

Most Modern Tragedy

is a product of

a disrespected Human Psyche.

The Modern Psyche

has been insidiously conditioned to

exclusively function at the pole of human

rationale

and remains hell-bent on rejecting the

existence and power

of the Subconscious Mind.

This headspace is wicked.

In this frame,

all morals are in flux

and all thoughts are

simply products of one's own Self.

Simply put,

everyone can be a hero

when morals are relative.

And no one can escape the possession

of a thought

when the Ego is paramount.

In this,

creating a true

Recipe for Disaster.

A Cry for Humanity

We've seen it.

We've seen the worst...

The worst to happen....yet.

We have seen the kids leave in fear

and the parents say goodbye.

We've seen the teachers become guardians,

while the parents wait on by.

We've seen the bulletproof backpacks

and the blood soaked snapbacks.

We've seen the schools become dangerous,

beyond a playground cry.

We've been forced to see them die.

We've been left to dry our own eyes.

But we never seem to seriously ask...

Why?

Why do we have to see them die?

Why is Evil so alive?

We've seen the great Divide.

The Divide so wide

that "great" doesn't even

capture its pride.

The Divide that makes us run

The Divide that makes us hide.

The Divide between family,

the Divide between friends.

The Divide between fathers

and their very own daughters.

The Divide between brothers,

and Life bearing mothers.

The Divide that began as moving

is now only inhuman.

This Divide

makes people die.

And that makes our people cry.

Why oh why is Evil so alive?

We've seen The Mask.

The Mask that covers the fat,

and hides the rat.

The Mask that projects perfection

and conjures rejection.

The Mask that fuels hate

and throws you the bait.

The bait of deception,

the bait of lies.

The bait of control,

the bait of disguise.

The bait of needing,

while constantly breeding

A reality of scorn,

A reality of hate.

A reality of deceit,

A reality of retreat.

A reality built on discontent.

A reality given to the human

hand to reinvent.

But why?

Why then is Evil so alive?

———————

This is not a howl,

but a cry.

This is not a

cry to justice,

nor a cry to law.

This not a cry for equality,

nor a cry for reform.

This a cry for all humanity.

This is

A cry for love.

A cry for all.

A cry to make things bright,

and a cry for The Eye that makes things

right.

The Eye that can see inside,

no matter how ugly it might be.

The Eye that can look forward,

no matter how dark it might be.

The Eye that can see the light of the Self

no matter how blinding it might be.

The Eye that can look back

no matter how distant it might be.

The I that can take responsibility.

The I that can accept defeat.

The I that can keep pushing forward.

The I that can take the heat.

The I that knows right.

The I that knows wrong.

The I that knows that it doesn't have very long.

Our lives are short.

Our lives are sweet.

Our lives are full of meaning,

no matter how badly you feel beat.

For we weren't born to die,

but to make a difference.

We weren't born to

breed evil,

but to

live for passion.

And passion lives

in what is respectable,

and in what is well.

And

Evil lives in

what is wicked,

and in the depths of hell.

This is not a yell,

but a cry.

A cry to Dive.

To Dive into zeal.

To Dive into love.

To Dive into darkness

and to free your own dove.

If we fail to Dive,

Evil will continue

to thrive.

So Dive.

Dive into the waters

of Life. Dive into the waters

of love.

Find meaning

to defy the hate.

Find meaning

to tolerate the pain.

It's about creation,

my friends,

not destruction.

Dive my dearest.

Dive to be alive.

In-site

True insight comes from a reality

that exists outside the bodily senses.

It exists somewhere else.

It exists in your heart.

Your heart often

confuses your Mind.

And that causes discomfort.

And for that reason alone,

you ignore it.

You toss it aside.

You force it to live in your dreams,

and there it stays,

begging you,

and only you,

to give it Life.

Give Life to your dreams.

Don't be rational.

That is not the time,

nor the place for exhausted rationality.

Real Talk

I might never find satisfaction in anything I do.

And if I do, that satisfaction will be temporary.

But for that I am thankful,

as satisfaction is the equalizer to growth.

And rarely has growth implied decay.

I can decay when I'm dead.

And so can you.

There will be plenty of time for that.

Worry's Route

We often listen to Worry.

Day in

and day out,

we listen to its Voice.

This Voice...

the Voice of Worry...

holds us back from what we can accomplish

and is

hellbent on chattering directly into our

ear.

How we worry is up to us.

We give it Life.

Worry is something that is created

for us, by us.

We know it's detrimental.

Yet,

we remain addicted to it.

We remain addicted to living in a state of frenzy.

―――――――

If you ever want to leave Worry behind,

you have to be the one to

buy the ticket,

punch it,

board the plane.

Only look back to learn from the place you used to be.

Irrational Missing Out

Our bodies are going to die.

Nobody makes it out of this Life alive.

It's one of the only things we really KNOW.

Although somehow,

through extreme arrogance and unwarranted ignorance,

we find ourselves living like we don't.

We live like we have postmortem "FOMO".

And that is a travesty.

As this way almost always leads to a Life

of preventing the present

to reach the future.

Until one day,

when that future never comes.

Remember,

Nobody makes it out alive.

Title X

The Mind is lost to the Soul on a nightly basis,

where it stays until the

Busy-Day tries its hardest

to track it down and reel it back in.

I-go

An unchecked Ego is the greatest agent of ignorance.

It will place a filter over your eyes;

a filter to blind you from the truth.

If left unmonitored for too long,

the Ego will become you,

and that's when trouble is born.

Because nobody can distort your perception better than yourSelf.

Freedom's Gatekeeper

Some days we live like a prisoner in an open cell.

We yell all day.

We yell all night.

Begging to be freed.

But the prison guard,

Sir Anxious Mind,

stands at the gate.

He's locked

and loaded,

waiting for our first step.

But we are too scared.

Too hesitant to change.

So we decide to stay another night.

"It's easier that way," we say with might.

Sooner than later,

that night turns into days.

And those days turn into months.

And we stay in that cell.

Waiting for the guard to budge.

We know he won't leave unless we make him.

But we wait anyways.

Hoping for a miracle.

If we're not careful,

If we never take that first step towards

the guard,

we might end up dying in that cell,

and if we do,

Freedom's somber tears will flood the cell

and escort our body

out.

Washing it away in a river of what could've been.

The Intuitive Plane

In order to articulate your own human experience,

you must feel Life on a different plane.

You don't have to spend all day there,

but at least pay it a visit

every once and awhile.

It's the place where you become extremely lucid and observant.

It's a place where your Life becomes a work of art.

It's where your Soul resides.

Waiting to be discovered.

Only you know where to find it.

And that's the easy part.

Getting there is the challenge.

United

The Hate derived from Argument

seems so futile when it is known that

The Argument is nothing more than

An Operation created by the existence of

You opposing You.

That is,

An Argument is simply A Message formulated

by

a unique conscious experience

being posed against

A Message of its exact same Nature,

thus dispelling the inherent Hate that is

attached to it.

There is nothing wrong with Argument,

In fact, Argument is necessary for growth.

But to see in this Light, and to see it

with this Eye, is to suddenly reveal a

Unification. Which, when we look at the world around US, seems to be one of our primary duties here on Earth.

Convenient Clarity

Without daily introspection and consideration of the culture around you,

what else is there to refine the Human Spirit?

Cravings From Existence

We need control.

When we have it,

we're fine.

When we don't,

we're not.

We lose control when

The Mind takes it from us.

And it takes it fast.

The Mind always invites his friend Worry too.

We can feel Worry coming in.

We can feel Worry crawling in our skin.

We envision Worry staying forever,

and that's when the extreme Anxiety sets in.

And then we ask,

"Is this Worry going to last forever?"

That,

my friends,

is officially being "out of control".

And the greatest thing about being out of control,

is that we can take control by knowing that we don't have much of it at all.

Full Moon

Risk is a tricky concept.

It strikes fear in the Mind

and Life in The Soul.

Without it we'd be living not to die; which

isn't living at all.

That's dying.

Dying means fading.

It means to fade away from this experience,

regardless of how fast your heart is

beating.

And living not to die

will make you fade away.

Don't fade,

Live.

Habit Mates

We are all bodies

of habit.

Habit is almost impossible to avoid.

But much like other things in this Life,

too much of it can kill

you.

It's important to monitor habit, but not

kick it to the curb

entirely.

You must find that elusive middle ground.

Living in habit is like riding on the back

of a motorcycle

driven by Time.

In order to get off of that motorcycle and

experience Life, one

must do something different each day.

Something that pushes you closer to the edge.

Something that makes you feel Life a bit deeper.

Something that makes the lives of others better.

Because in the end,

that's the goal.

To leave this place better than you found it.

To make your mark,

not in a notorious manner,

but one that will be remembered in euphoria because of You.

How 2 Surf

It's important to remain calm when waves of anxiety come

rolling in.

Instead of diving in and getting tossed around,

stay on your board and watch how they break.

Study their patterns.

Master their tricks.

Only then will you be able to surf.

Complicated Simplicity

Being a part of this world is hard.

It's not for the feint of heart.

Life is like being locked in a small closet

with a truck

load of wasps and a bottle of bug spray.

You can use as much repellent as you'd

like,

but eventually the sting of Life

will prove to be too much and

push you over the edge.

The only way to survive is to open the

door.

The door that is right in front of

you.

But many of us won't notice the door,

for it would be far too easy

to be the real solution.

───────────

It doesn't have to be difficult

to be optimal.

Haze-y

Finding a purpose in Life is special.

It's one of those things that lifts the veil from

in front of your eyes,

revealing a brand new world.

It reveals a beautiful existence that was hidden behind a layer

of thick smoke.

That moment is great.

But what is even greater is

knowing that it can happen more than once.

F.E.A.R (False E-mages Appearing Real)

The true danger in social media exists in the simple fact that it can be controlled.
People can cultivate any image they desire.
The problem is that WE don't see through that.
All we do is See it. Read it. And Believe it.
Then,
due to our own Self-consciousness,
feel bad about ourselves.
And to the best of our abilities,
we engage in the same process to make ourselves feel sufficient.
Thus, creating the dirty,
vicious cycle of our times.

On a bus

To change the world,

you have to create something that is

crazy enough to catch

and obscure enough to stick around.

Diet

Fleeing sleep in pursuit of a dream is one of the greatest adventures a person can find.

Reflection of Vanity

When evil rises out of the sea,

Life is given to the bourgeoisie.

We ask "who gave that man a machete."

We shout "this is not how it's suppose to be!"

But we never seem to ask:

"Is that evil just an extension of me?"

And it is in this very scope,

that it can be seen

how The World is driven to violence and terror

by the very thing that

The Individual is scared

to FIND within oneSelf.

Work?

When the line that separates work and leisure can be blurred and you find yourSelf truly happy,

you know you are in the right place.

For now.

LoVe

What makes love so elusive?

What makes love so grand?

The answer,

my friend,

is Love's power to transcend.

It's Love's power to defy the laws of this land.

If we look close enough, we can catch a

glimpse of how

Love defines the laws of perception,

forcing us to make every exception.

For if love is real,

It always holds true,

that the greater the distance

the stronger the glue.

Love is still there

when the heartbeat is lost.

Love is still strong

when this Life is gone.

And something that strong

isn't here for no reason.

The reason for love is elusive

and grand.

It's one that we might never understand.

But its reason for living;

even when the body is dead,

is simply

the act of waiting for the

heart to mend.

Tragedy

Just show up.

Even if you don't feel like it.

If you continue to show up,

it becomes a habit,

and habits change lives.

And when Life is changed by the power of

the habit of showing up, it becomes a

philosophy,

and philosophy is solid.

It won't crumble in

the face of disaster.

It won't fail in

times of need.

And in times of tragedy,

nothing is more important

than knowing you can rely on something within yourSelf.

Just show up.

Even when you don't feel like it.

The Test

Death is certain.

Life is not.

Death is the test,

and Life is the preparation.

The test's subject is known,

but what questions will be asked have

flown.

The only way to know

what is on the test

is to take it.

So prepare.

Read. Learn.

Mediate. Meditate.

Prepare yourSelf.

And when it's your time

to take the test,

trust in your ability.

Trust in your preparation.

All things must pass.

And your test is no

exception.

The Life-belt

When you're anxious about something,
half the battle is knowing what that thing
is. The rest is like fastening a seatbelt.

Pull too hard
and the belt will tense up,
leaving you no option but to
return to the place you started and
pull again.

The idea is to pull it slow;
to pull it smooth.
To pay attention to the journey,
and the little details that move.

Worried 4 Worry

Sometimes a worry is only

a worry because it's foggy.

You can see pieces of it,

but the full picture is not clear. And that

worries us.

It makes us uncomfortable.

And we're human.

Humans don't like worry.

Humans despise chaos.

So humans worry.

The problem with worry

is that it never makes the picture clearer.

It only makes it worse.

It only makes us blind.

To make the picture clear

and quiet the worry,

we must first recognize that

the picture is indeed foggy.

And in that,

we can begin moving towards a psychic space where

the picture will become clear.

WHO DO YOU LOVE?

One-Eyed-Blind

This Life,

this experience,

is One in Two.

It is the overprotective parent

and the wide-eyed child.

It is the ambitious dreamer

and the repressing realist.

On their own,

these personalities are

destined for disaster.

These personalities

run sure until

it's too late.

And that's why You exist.

To mediate.

To keep them from going too far.

To keep them existing in harmony

and in alignment.

To know this

is to see

the illusion of limitation.

To apply this

is to free

yourSelf from the chains of illusion.

Enlighten your being.

Lift the illusion.

And see the truth.

Memories on Grand

Pure truth exists

in things and ideas

that feel like a memory

but were never experienced

on this Earth.

The Willfully Blind

Opportunity is thrown at your feet

in simply realizing that

a lot of *what* you fear

are only false presuppositions

and a lot of *who* you fear

are only alternative versions

of yourSelf.

State of Division

Much of your pain is

a product of repression.

Not by society,

but by yourSelf.

We must learn to release the Ego,

and

let our Souls run free.

I don't know about you,

but that's where I want to be.

Problems, child

You need problems.

Problems keep you alive.

Problems keep you living.

Call them problems,

but they're also goals.

Call them a burden,

but they're also a gift.

For the reward isn't in the solution,

but the solving.

Trick of Dreams

It is amazing to watch the

seismic shift that happens

when you

stop using the word "dream"

and start using the word "intention".

Places Beyond Perception

When you are looking for something,

close your eyes and listen.

That is where the answer is.

That is where the truth is.

And truth is the key ingredient to

gaining insight.

Just See:

Sight is deceptive.

Insight is truthful.

Remember:

Everything

You think

Now, in this moment,

One Day, Might

Leave you

Dead; In

Search of something new.

EMPTY ROOM

Regret Has no chance

to live

if what you give

is nothing short

of your all.

1thru9

The body is

a vessel for translation.

The Soul is

a vessel for transcendence.

Leave

There comes a point

in every relationship

where the devastation from holding on

shrinks at the hands of

the freedom in letting go.

To notice this shift and take it

is emancipating.

But to notice it and throw it away

is toxic.

Compassionate Empathy

While opening your eyes to see is daring,

getting behind someone else's eyes is

courageous.

For it requires empathy

and empathy is scary.

It's scary because it's real;

and that's reality.

In this frame,

reality is humbling to even the most

prosperous.

For it reveals that you are them,

and they are you.

All Aboard

Any single thing in this Life

can be defined as a ride.

No matter how grand the stage

or how subtle circumstance,

anything that acts is a ride.

Approach each ride

as something totally wild.

To do this is to accept the gift of Life.

Stand Under to Understand

There are things that

are simply meant to be.

For how else would you be free?

Masque

Lose your smile.

How do you feel?

If the answer doesn't *change*,

then *change* is your answer.

Real-al-ity

If more people knew

how many people are trying to keep it

together while

it all falls apart,

this Life

and

these days

would serve

this dimension

a lot closer to

what is needed.

Juggernauts of Society

Never mess with a slow-driver.

For the ability to drive slow requires one

of two things:

Either an extreme sense of confidence

or a defiant lack of Self-awareness.

The slow driver can be either of these

things,

but not both.

And to mess with a person that possesses

either one of these

skills is the ultimate

act of futility.

There are slow drivers everywhere in this world.

Pass wisely.

Unchecked Aggression

Impulses run deep.

So deep that they go unnoticed.

Without being inspected,

Impulses can suck us beneath the surface

and leave us to die.

Not physically.

But spiritually.

Our bodies remain,

but our Mind suffers.

Be weary of impulses.

A Life lived via impulse is a Life

unexamined.

When you develop the ability to be aware

of your own impulses,

you will unlock a world you have never seen before.

Some things will be beautiful.

Some ugly.

But most things will have meaning.

And that is the divinity that we are looking for.

Whether we know it or not.

Focus

We humans want to do it all.

But the crazy part of wanting to do it all

is that we end up doing

nothing at all.

<u>U</u>

To stick a word like "I"

with one definition would be much like

trying to keep a goldfish

dry and alive.

Think about it.

It makes sense.

But don't think too hard.

That forces Wisdom to flee.

Constraint? Perhaps

Time is a tool created by man.

A tool that keeps everyone in line.

It places limits on what we THINK we can do.

It places limits on how we act,

and how we function.

When boiled down,

time places parameters on how we live.

Time was created by us.

And anything created by us has true

potential to be

detrimental to us,

without us noticing it.

Take advantage of Time,

or let it take advantage of You.

Racing

Be careful when chasing something.

The race starts fast.

And when it does,

it's filled with excitement.

Determination flows deep,

and you are moving towards something

you want to meet.

However,

without constant insight or reflection

the race can kill you.

So be careful.

Don't let the race you're running hide its

finish-line without you noticing.

Because that leaves you with no option but

to chase a point

you've already passed.

And then,

you'll be running forever,

in a race with no end.

Get Lost Loss

Loss cannot be escaped.

To escape losing in this world is like running from your own

pulse.

The harder you try the more intense the

presence gets.

Eventually it will stop.

One time for good.

In order to live,

we must get to know loss.

And work with it,

instead of against it.

Mainstream

In you,

there is a rope.

Like most,

this rope has two ends.

Like few,

this rope pierces and runs directly

through your Soul.

And like all,

this rope can pull you up

or

it can pull you down.

The good thing about this rope is that it's

You that exists on both ends.

The bad thing about this rope is that it

means your actions *matter*.

For in finding your Rope,

you see that

You are the only one in charge of

which end is going to be pulled.

Purified Solvent

Anxiety becomes useless when perception becomes autonomous.

Think about that next time you are online.

It's ok....

A wakening

Being used by the internet is common.

More common than we think.

It makes you feel good in the moment.

But only for that moment.

Then, like a classy escort,

the internet leaves you lying there alone.

Sad, alone, and strung-out;

looking for more.

?What?

Truth without insight is a deception.
There is nothing that says the highest
value exists in what we
see with our eyes.

To believe such a thing
makes Life stiff.
And that's hard.
And Life's hard enough.

Stay limber.

Undercover and Overgrown

You are a jewel hiding in the tall weeds.

Weeds that were planted by both society and the Ego.

These weeds can be cut down,

but only by you.

And the longer you wait,

the harder it is going to get out.

Start now.

A Secret

Sleep is a pure form of sacrifice.

Sleep is your Mind letting your Body enter

its most vulnerable

state; completely open to the world.

Sleep is your Subconscious allowing your

nerves to calm down and

your brain to release its governor.

Sleep makes way for The Dreamer.

The Dreamer arrives when The Realist is

calm enough to open the

door.

This is a great discovery in Life,

that when applied to the conscious state,

acts as the pinnacle source of inspiration.

Open the door

and make way for The Dreamer.

Then listen and watch,

as The Dreamer takes over

and your Life becomes clear.

In Hiding

Only with the right kind of eyes

will Omens appear.

Omens come in all forms.

Forms of good and

forms of evil.

Some will lead to bliss.

Others to despair.

Standing alone an Omen is weak.

But once you string them together, they

begin to gain power.

At a certain point, these Omen-strings

become powerful enough to

shatter your world or energize your Soul.

It's up to you,

the Viewer,

to choose which Omens to follow.

Will you follow the Omens to an existence of infinite

inspiration?

Or will you follow the Omens to an existence of endless fear?

Both are there.

Waiting on their taker.

And their taker,

is You.

GR8ful

It's rare to find a young person in the right place.

And if they are indeed in that right place, they should be grateful.

Most people never get there.

Just ask around,

the face won't lie.

__Thought 1__

The rate of violence in the world today is unsettling.
Violence can be a last ditch effort in trying to control that which can't be.

Senseless.

Worst of all,
any act of violence always holds potential to harm the innocent.
And when it does,
violence becomes truly unique.
As it remains one of the
only things in this Life that can truly exceed devastation
and definition.

Don't slip

Don't rush through this Life.

Rushing forces you to miss the good.

And sometimes,

that good only happens once

and then it's lost.

If you wish to rush,

Rush through social media.

That can always be tracked down.

Liberation

The world was not created for the human senses.

The human senses were created for the world.

True power exists in realizing the limits of your own senses,

and seeing what exists beyond.

Once that journey is underway,

A force is activated,

And The Soul is revealed.

And that Soul can't be taken from you,

not even by the hands of Death.

And that,

my friend,

is true power.

Life's Path

The path of Life.....

We're all on it together.

We're all walking towards something.

We think we know where we are going.

We think we know where this path leads to.

But really,

nobody knows.

And that's what keeps us walking.

Because if we did,

Life itSelf would lose its purpose.

__Your Competition__

Nobody likes to come in second place to a phone.

Especially when you are lying next to the person you care about.

For then too much becomes too clear too fast.

It's at this moment that it's known

that the person next to you

isn't just lying with you,

but lying to you.

En-er-gy

You can only run from your problems for so

long before they

catch you.

And when they do,

You will be ready for them.

For you will know

that a problem's Life is

solely dependent on the energy you supply

it.

Be Selfish.

Take that energy back

and watch.

Not only will you be able to run again,

but you'll be able to run free again.

Look Here!

Decision is vital to peace of Mind.

It's the base of all Self-authority.

What you like about yourSelf is your

decision.

And that feels good.

But what feels even better

is recognizing that what you don't like

about yourSelf is also

your decision.

Meaning that change can happen at the snap

of your own

two fingers.

All you have to do is decide.

It's that cool.

Possession

Don't sacrifice what you have for something you don't.

The past is gone.

The future is abstract.

But the present is YouRS.

And that is exactly what it is.

A present.

Treat it that way.

Lost in Plasticity

The jungle of material items is a dubious place.

If you don't stop and look back, you'll get lost.

And once lost,

the only way back is to ask:

"Is what others see of me a complete stranger to who I know I am?"

And only when you find your answer to that question,

will you know how to get back home

and navigate your way through the jungle.

Thoughts on 1st Street

Few spaces are worse than knowing you're being used,

but acting like you're not.

Willpower

It's not about what kind of water you let through,

but whether you decide to drink it or not.

If you can think or not.

Maybe it's time to blink a lot.

But but knows?

This isn't a Manifesto.

Holding Sanity

Questioning reality is the only way to make

sure we stay sane.

If we move along in the same routine for

too long,

things stop changing.

And in an ever changing world,

That's insane.

Hey, Buddy....

Life becomes easy(ier) when you become who you are.

The hard part is finding yourSelf.

You could be anywhere.

Hiding in any opportunity.

In any place.

Except the internet.

You're not there.

Manuel 4 U

Only when you start to risk your Life will you unlock the instructions on how to live.

It's not going to be safe.

No matter how hard you try.

It never was

and it never is.

This world is hard on people.

Risk isn't.

The Drink

You can't drink to 'get away'.

One day you'll come back to yourSelf and

the reason you left in

the first place will still be there,

waiting to be fixed.

If you never come back,

the simple thought of returning will live

with you forever.

And that will kill you.

Ambulances

Ambulances are packed with perspective.

They signify that someone is in need.

They signify struggle.

They signify death.

Ambulances serve as the universal icon of mortality.

But I've grown to like them.

I see them as a reminder.

A simple symbol of our fate.

Which is death.

On any given day,

whatever problems I am dealing with

are extinguished at the sight of an ambulance.

My consciousness shifts.

It shifts into a space that forces me to be grateful.

Grateful that the person in need is getting helped

and

grateful that the person isn't me.

Yet.

The Living Kind

Every person you meet

has the power to change your Life.

How they change your Life is usually up to you.

But every once in awhile,

if you are lucky,

you get the chance to meet someone so authentic and full of passion,

that you have no option but to say "thank you" to whoever it is

you give "thanks" to.

For once this "someone" has entered your Life,

Life itself has no option but to get better.

I was lucky once.

I met a girl.

She was one of these types...
The Living Kind.

She was

so cool and

so real

I was sure it was a dream.

And a person like her is not only hard to find,

but admirable beyond the reaches of The Mind.

I am sure I will never meet another person like her.

And that's a good thing.

For a Shooting Star is both beautiful and rare.

And this girl,

without a doubt,

is just that.

If you ever meet someone like this,

don't blink.

Or you might miss them.

And once they've left,

the only thing that will be left

is the chatter around you,

describing the Magic that once was.

Thoughts Vol. 1

With the right eyes,

things start to make sense.

Some of these things will appear beautiful,

but most,

due to the mask worn by our own concrete

sense of reality,

will be terrifying.

It's difficult to wake up to yourSelf.

But don't stop trying.

You'll arrive.

Red Velvet

Only when you gain the ability to identify

The Soul

can you deal with your own deceptive fears.

For when you are in touch with your Soul,

matters of mere reality will fall limp

to matters of mere mortality.

And when you confront your own mortality,

most of your fears will dissolve in front

of your eyes.

It's not magic,

but a trick.

Do You--

Wonder why you eat all the right things but can't lose weight??... think about it Lad, but don't ask The Dietician.

Wonder why you have all these insane ideas that have nothing to to do with who you are??... think about it Lad, but don't ask The Humanities.

Wonder why you wake up angry and go to bed drunk? Think about it Lad... but don't ask the Professor.

Wonder why you change your outfits three times before taking a shower?? Think about it Lad... but don't ask your Best Friend.

Wonder why everything that you want seems to belong to someone else?? Think about it Lad... but don't ask the Curator.

Wonder why that cough you had has suddenly put you in a hospital bed??... Think about it Lad, but don't ask The Internet.

Wonder why you want to cause pain to your Neighbor? Think about it Lad... but don't ask The Priest.

Wonder why you have a strong scorn for anyone who challenges your Sight??... think about it Lad, but don't ask your Eyes.

Wonder why you feel like the Anxious State defines this dimension??... think about it Lad, but don't ask The Ego.

I's

If something is true,

it usually remains

when the eyes are closed.

Boundless

If the Mind has yet to frighten the Self,

then the Mind is still sleeping.

Deeper and Deeper

To take on a symbol that is a

product of the Divine

is to accept a gift

from God

and turn the internal Soul into

a place of refuge.

Anyone can discount a symbol

on the basis of "reason".

But once one does that,

they're forced to recognize

the truths

that are still standing strong.

And

therein is the fusion point

between opposites.

Proclamation Eight-78

To my left is a great fire,

to my right,

a well stacked world.

As I stand in the middle,

meditating the two worlds in

the form of a Human Body,

I know that The Soul that brought me here

is not of this world

or any human hand,

but,

like anything on this Earth,

requires its opposite in order to exist.

In this Life,

The Soul is grounded in the human hand.

And the human hand, grounded in The Soul.

And when in harmony,

the two work

to experience and communicate

what is known but has yet to be discovered.

The Divine Knight

I suppose if this Life is indeed a magical game,

then it's

a metaphysical chess match between that of which can and can't be controlled.

And in this game,

you and me are no more a Piece than the Player.

We are no more The Knight than The Hand that moves it.

And that's the great paradox.

The only way to have real control in this Life is to take notice and place faith in The Hand we cannot see.

If a Knight plays the Game by himSelf,

as himSelf,

his options for movement are limited.

Yet and still,

this manages to be the very least of the

tragedies that occur when one tries to play

the Game as the Game.

The real tragedy hits when the Knight looks around and

sees the Other Pieces.

Pieces that can do what he cannot.

Pieces that can move where he cannot.

The Knight knows,

deep in his heart,

that as long as he exists as The Knight,

the other pieces will stay put.

Their potential will be

bottled in place.

In this,

The Knight discovers

the need

to place his faith

in The Hand,

and allow The Hand to move the Pieces as One.

Then and only then

will The Knight move in Harmony

with the rest of the board,

and be granted the keys

to his own true potential.

Behind the Curtain

The more we think

we know something,

the more familiar it gets.

And the more familiar a thing is,

the less potency it has.

Maybe that's why

the rate of

unNatural Disasters

is on the rise.

YTOT

The pain of embarrassment

is harsh.

But that pain is nothing

compared to the pain of

not being yourSelf.

And when one evades

the Self through

the Fear of embarrassment,

the Truth becomes harder to see,

as you are voluntarily subjecting yourSelf

to

Possession

by what You Think Others Think.

Ain't Pop

Your Power in all situations,

whether it be a

    fit of Anxiety,

        a run-in with Depression,

            or a rendezvous with Bliss,

rarely exists outside

of the Present Moment.

Tied in The Field

Only in the Syzygies

will we find Reality,

and only in Reality will

we find lies.

Working

Ego Consciousness will forever

be One's greatest battle.

It

questions the guiding light of the Soul

at all costs.

Conformity in its name is nothing

to be ashamed of.

But let it be known,

that if you wish to figure out why you're

here,

it must be fought.

It All Comes Back

Life is a Gift.

And

To fear Death

is to expose one of our the greatest

weaknesses:

The ignorance of that which hasn't

been earned.

Revel

Amazing things will happen

when you begin to realize

the true significance

contained in

visions that exists before

the closed eyes.

1:02am

Do you find it odd that something as intrinsic as TIME is rooted in an entity that doesn't require it?

Green Five Minus

If we are to consider the fact

that all movements that occur

on Earth are subjected to and

operate within the same set of laws,

it's hard not to look at its *Harmonious*

Existence

as a *guide* from the Divine.

In nature,

it's observable that each thing requires

its opposite to exist.

Death requires Life,

just as

Light requires Dark.

In these relationships,

it's clear that their sheer polarity

creates a Balance

that allows for its existence

in *Harmony*.

Being that Life and Nature were indeed given to us,

it can be looked at as a gift,

and because it is a gift,

it can be expected that We,

due to our intrinsic tendency to

de-value that which isn't earned,

might overlook Nature's all but obvious

message on how it is we can look inside ourselves

and find a space that creates

an

Existence of Harmony.

XROADS

When You find it to be only You that

stands in the way of the Life you want,

You can be sure You have arrived.

You can look around,

and what you see is a

Peculiar Crossroads.

A Crossroads

that consists of You and You.

                                        You vs. You.

You are both.

You are the One who called

and

        the One who answered.

You are the One who took off running

and

      the One who was waiting.

You are both the Creator

and

      the Consumer.

You are both The Saint

and

      The Devil.

And it is at this Crossroads,

that you will find it *possible* to

discover

your True Potential for Good

and

your True Potential for Evil.

And while this Place is perhaps the thing

you have

been waiting on your entire Life,

it also becomes a great commitment.

For once it's known,

The Blame will

rarely exist Outside again.

Nightflow

If there is something to be believed,

ask to see its Opposite.

If its Opposite doesn't exist in the field

of vision,

or remains hidden from the Mind,

then we must search.

It is only in the fusion of the opposites

that we are able to Grow

beyond this Space we call

Here and Now.

A Note to Those Who Want It

The Soul desires

sovereignty over the Mind and the body.

When that desire is unfulfilled,

anxiety becomes stronger,

worry becomes a reality,

and reality gets dark.

This isn't something new.

It has always been true.

Even if you never knew,

that only You

can change You.

Fulfill your Soul and

the rest will align.

The Truth

What do you see when you close your eyes?

What do you hear in the sound of silence?

What do you feel when you are all alone?

The answer;

The Truth.

The Truth is realized.

The Truth is known.

The Truth shall never be owned.

And

The rest is confusion.

Full-Circle

IF YOU'RE GOING TO TAKE SOMETHING,

WORK FOR IT.

THAT IS THE ONLY RIGHT WAY TO

TAKE IT.

ANYTHING OTHER THAN THAT IS STEALING.

AND STEALING ALWAYS COMES BACK TO BITE.

IN THIS LIFE

OR THE NEXT.

In the Nightfall

The Powerful Man

is only powerful

to a certain splinter of people.

The Wise Man is consistent

amongst all.

All U Have

Live here.

Live now.

Listen to Life.

Listen to The Soul.

Take into account what The Soul has to say;

realize how special it is

to be in conversation with it.

Realize how special it is

to hear whispers from a metaphysical

reality.

And be thankful when the whispers define

the falsity

that has been created for you,

by you.

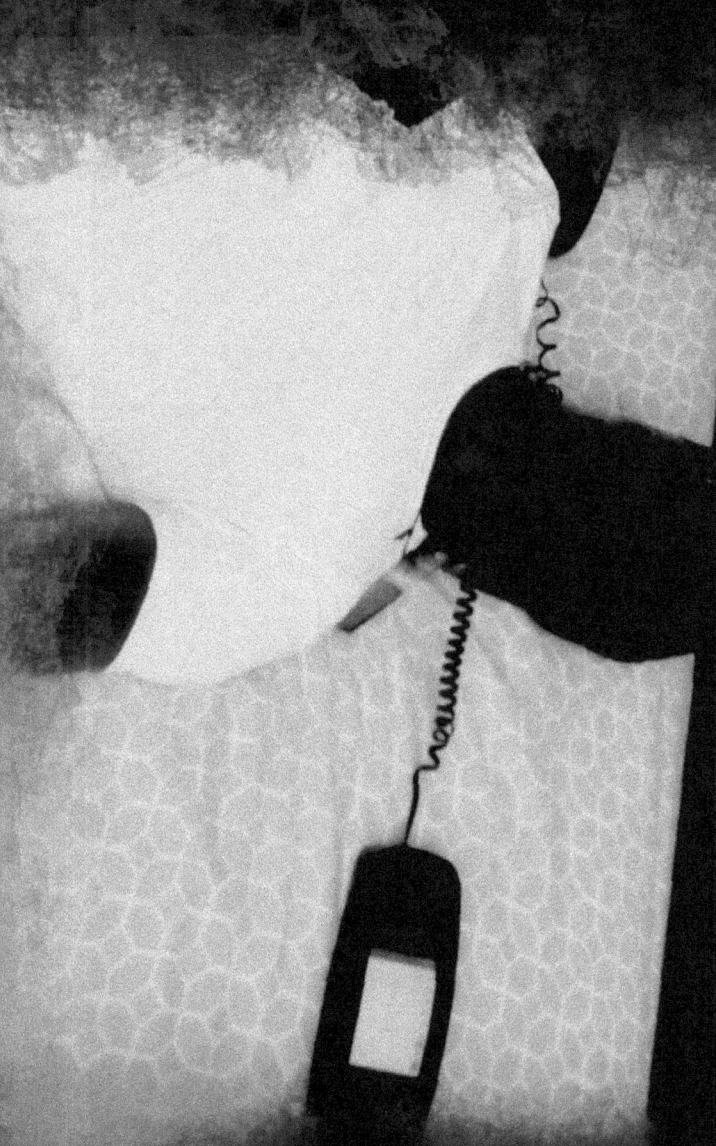

ON HIGH

When things begin to change in meaning

but remain consistent in their shape,

you can be sure you're waking up to

something.

For it is then you realize that everything

you've been told

originated in a Conscious

no different than what's accessible to you.

And

NOW YouR HIGH.

Dissolved

When you listen

you will find the truth.

When you ignore

you will live in lie,

despite the words you say.

Without Pain

When the pain is too great

to be meaningless,

It has no other option

but to be a part of your plan.

It's here to teach you.

And you're here to teach US.

Conscious of the Unconscious

Becoming conscious

of the Subconscious Mind

holds great potential to

solve your most

troublesome problems.

While it takes courage to search,

it won't take long

to find,

and once discovered,

it must be trusted.

Not because it's always right,

but because the knowledge of

all those who came before you

is now in your hands.

Be careful.

In Order to Get Somewhere

Any day spent in a fog should be noted,

and if that fog hangs around,

it's time to wipe your eyes

and look inside yourSelf.

There is no such thing as clarity

when dealing with illusion.

And illusion is indeed an "ill-state-of-Mind"

only to be relieved by listening to

your own heart.

57 and Nic

Look inside.

There you will find a thing.

An idea that feels familiar,

but remains hidden from sight.

A feeling of knowing,

that tells you it's right.

That's Desire.

It's your Purpose looking for the light.

The only way to find it is to follow your heart.

All you must do is give it a chance to start.

D

  E

   E

    P

The Mind will bend to the Soul's desires
if the Soul can make its way through.

While this truth is indeed a fright,
its liberation is limitless.

It gives warrant to The Dreamer
and inflicts fear in The Realist,
as the impossibility of the realm we call
Reality
dissolves into the abyss it originated
from.

Cloudy I's

If your truth becomes untrue when this moment becomes anew...then you must know that you got it from somewhere you should have never knew.

The Cycle of Success

Success in anything

always comes down to

work, discipline, and

a dash of luck.

The dash of luck only works

when you are prepared.

And preparation requires

discipline and work.

Thus, creating

The Cycle of Success.

The Smoke

The Incense Stick is no mistake.

For if the Stick itSelf is The Totality of Time,

Then the burning ember is Time itSelf.

In this scope,

it can be seen that

We are all simply a space on The Stick,

waiting for the burning ember to grace us

with the fiery energy

of Life,

and when it does,

we not only receive the opportunity of a

Lifetime,

but also accept the notion that

we will be transformed into

The Smoke.

The Smoke is a place where disturbance is

noted

and all Force is exposed,

for The Smoke is an

Entity that tells no lies.

And

contained in The Smoke that is present in

the Third

lives the Spirit of those in the Fourth.

Effort

I wish

you knew how hard you were trying

to avoid being the person

you are.

(Me)dia

In the same way the food you eat shapes

your body,

the media you consume

shapes your Mind.

And yet,

we continue to wonder why we live

in such an anxious society.

Little Adjustments

Take note of the day's happenings.

Notice what worked.

But more importantly,

notice what didn't.

For

how do you expect to grow

if you continue to rely

on the same memories?

4 You

Be aware of the guidelines you set for yourSelf.

If you are not where you want to be, perhaps those guidelines need to be revised.

Or quite simply forgotten.

Always make sure you have lines to guide you.

If you don't, you will live a Life of oppression.

Oppression given to you by the hands of your own unchecked emotions.

And much like trying to hide from fear, unchecked emotions always end in disaster.

Relax

There is great liberation

to be discovered

in giving up the

insidious need to always

"BE RIGHT".

Look In, Not Right

Once you realize who you are,

you can stop sacrificing

for the Self you were searching for.

This will not only free up new energy for

growth and expansion of the real you,

but perhaps allow you to stay awake for the

good stuff.

Xcess

The things we desire in excess

are designed to destroy us.

In most cases,

Moderation is key.

It's where you need to be.

Don't let these things carve a future out

for you.

Rather,

use these things as tools

to carve a future for yourSelf.

Fitness

And then we must ask,

at what point will evolution value

the ability to unlock a phone over the

ability to walk.

More importantly,

what will that do

to our ability to walk?

Law

If stealing an identity is a crime,

check yourSelf.

And if you're indeed guilty,

you better walk yourSelf out

of the courthouse before

the judge slams

the gavel

and sentences you to Life.

Fleeing from Proximity

To discover more about "you"

you must loosen the reins of conscious

desire.

That guarantees a thrust into The Unknown,

and The Unknown is the only place

that is known

to outline your true identity, test it, and

refine it for proper growth.

Vacation Destination

Some people love the beach,

while others love the wide open sea.

Both places are free to be.

But you,

my friend,

will only be free

in the high tide of

the wide open sea.

Don't Worry. This Won't Hurt.

If we don't have any regrets,

we are not risking enough.

We must stay limber.

Risk is where Life lives.

And in order to live,

you have to find your way

through Risk.

Dr. Soul and Mr. Brain

The Soul is given

a Brain to articulate its intuition.

The Soul is given

a Brain to articulate what it already

knows.

The accuracy of these articulations

depends on how strong the connection

between

the two are.

Only you can bring them together.

Only you can make them sing.

The Sole

The sole attached to the body greets the

dirtiest

places the Earth has to offer,

while the Soul living in the body

greets the dirtiest thoughts

the Mind has to offer.

Both are necessary to existence,

but without the Soul,

the sole has no purpose at all.

Go.

If you feel the need to travel,

or GO,

then just go.

Thought is useful,

but too much can lead to indecision.

And indecision

is a destination for the stagnant.

And nothing will halt travel faster than

subterranean stagnation.

Abuse

Distorted mortality is an agent of

of addiction.

It's not responsible for all,

for addiction is a disease.

However,

understanding mortality in the

presence of death

can reveal what is truly important in Life.

And sadly,

what we find when we peel back these layers

are the people and things that are

hurt the most at the hands

of Addiction.

That is no coincidence.

Stoplights

Stoplights are peculiar things.

Circular, Colored lights that control our lives.

Without thinking,

Without knowing,

We obey.

And it works.

Stoplights keep order,

but only because we listen.

Life has stoplights too.

They're hard to see,

but easy to feel.

Most of the time we feel them

without recognizing it.

Sometimes we go on RED,

Even though we know it's wrong.

We get away with it for awhile,

but eventually we crash,

and everything we once knew

is broken.

Yet,

what is even worse than going on RED,

is stopping on GREEN.

We will sit at a green light,

in some cases,

FOREVER.

Just waiting.

Waiting for something to happen,

or someone to help.

Waiting for another signal.

But the light is GREEN,

And that's as far as the Universe is going

to

take it.

The rest of the work is up to you.

You never know where you

might arrive

if you put your foot on the gas

and drive.

Riches

The gold isn't always hiding at the end of

the rainbow.

That's just what we're told.

In Life,

The gold is scattered.

It's stashed away in everything.

It's in everyone.

Even you.

It's your duty to find it,

and dig it up.

If you start looking

for gold,

you will become rich.

Rich in a currency that

nobody can take away from you.

And that's true wealth.

The Rain

I had to pull over.

I had to pull over

because of the rain.

Not the rain on my windshield,

but the rain in my eyes.

I started to sink.

I sank deeper and deeper,

until my head

was under.

I could not breathe.

I could not see.

I was losing grip on who I thought

was Me.

I was running out of breath,

running out of Life.

I started to swim.

I didn't know where I was going,

but I knew it was right.

I reached the surface

And I got that next breath.

The breath that brought me back.

The breath that gave me Life.

Whenever you find yourSelf underwater,

Keep swimming.

And swim with courage.

Swim with strength.

Not because you want to,

but because you have to.

Because that next breath is there.

It's waiting for you.

It's waiting to give you Life.

No matter how deep you sink,

Keep swimming.

Peek at the Future

One of the best ways to learn about yourSelf

is to look at your parents.

It's like reading a pre-game report,

except in this game,

you're playing,

not watching.

You have some control over the outcome.

It's your responsibility.

Find You

There is still a lot of You

out there.

There is still a lot of You

to be *found*,

      discovered,

and   *loved*.

But most importantly,

there is still a lot of You

to be *lived*.

The BASE. Looking up

When you're standing at the base of a

climb,

it's always better to go up

than to

walk away.

The shame of not trying is usually

worse than anything that could

happen to you up there.

Our Role Model

Whoever finds good sense

in a thing that

doesn't make any

is the person we desire to be.

Looking for TRUTH

If the thing you are looking for

is meant to be found

and understood completely,

then maybe it's not

the one you want.

Keep searching.

E(vil)

Evil will destroy you before

you can,

for

Evil is insidious at Heart.

Evil is everywhere.

You can't flee,

or it will follow.

You distance yourSelf from Evil

by standing steady and holding your ground.

And

you destroy Evil

by recognizing your own capacity to do the

same.

Satisfy

Progress...

It starts with sacrifice

and ends with satisfaction.

To sacrifice now,

is to ensure that

satisfaction is

there at the end,

no matter when your exit may be.

Diamonds

Many times

what holds us back is

not a lack of *ambition*,

but a lack of *assurance*.

If whatever exists at the end

of any adventure

is unclear or unstable,

we choose not to start at all;

missing the entire trip.

We deem it not worth the effort,

not worth the time.

But how can something lack value

if its worth is still buried?

While in the pursuit of any goal,

it's always about the digging.

For a diamond would be

worthless without its miner.

To Look

Don't confuse Sight

with Vision.

To look is easy,

but to see is hard.

We look at things,

but we see the truth.

And when you see the truth,

a lot of what is around you

will vanish.

Destination Dorado

Your destination might distort,

leaving you wondering *where*?

Your reality might vanish,

leaving you wondering *what*?

But as long as your *why* remains living,

your direction will be clear,

and when on the journey of Life,

direction is all that is necessary.

No Matter What You Do

It is far better to die while living

than to live while dying.

Virtue 4 U

The quiet Mind is a virtue.

When your Mind is quiet

you can hear the truth.

The rest of it is like a garage sale.

It's Rare Gold surrounded by

garbage.

Don't listen to pass the time.

Listen to hear.

Don't listen to respond.

Listen to learn.

I New a Knew Thing Once

The extra dose of Joy

we get from *sharing* a profound experience

is a simple metaphysical orientation.

It's a sign that we might be on the right path.

It's a signal that we might be traveling on the common road of the human race.

The one that leads us to our common goal of

One Love.

Three-15

Live through the Spirit,

emit the Divine.

Then,

and only then,

will your Soul be fine.

3:17

To shun the Spirit

is to pronounce inspiration dead....

regardless of how fast your

heart is beating.

...Skyline?

We should ask ourselves this:

Is it better for me to sail in circles,

and avoid the impending waterfall?

Or

sail towards the edge and

find out where it is?

3.18

If something is rude

it's usually true.

Burial Ground

One that is buried by the powers of Habit

and Anxiety

is buried by themSelves.

Habit and Anxiety have the power to de-rail

a person's Life

on their own.

When combined and given the chance to run

free,

Habit and Anxiety will

become the Storm with No Eye.

Recognize that The Storm with No Eye

will knock the roof off your house

with relentless effort;

with countless attempts.

It's your job to create the Eye.

You must be the Eye.

You must know the Eye.

And

as long as you have your Eye,

you can always find your way back to the

Calm and build a new home.

Real Wealth

If the

best things in Life are free.

Then

Time is the greatest currency.

Faith

Few things in this Life are impossible.

Freedom without a form of Faith is one of them.

Building Your Home

The place is hard.

Bad, horrible, and tragic things

are GOING to happen.

It is that simple.

Trying to ignore that fact

makes it even worse.

For then you're lying to yourSelf.

And when you lie to yourSelf enough times,

you start to believe.

And with belief,

comes euphoria,

and with euphoria

comes desire for more.

Then,

your own lies start to stack;

much like a house of cards.

And while a house of cards is

pleasing to the eye,

its foundation is weak.

All it takes is a simple breath

to make it come crashing down.

Blissful Self Tragedy

To avoid suffering

is to avoid Life.

And to avoid Life

while trying to live

is tragic.

Search

The allure of Curiosity

is the lure of Change.

Who knows?

It might not be Death

that is to be feared,

but rather the thought of Death

subjecting you to an infinite existence

of the Life you're living right now.

I, my friend, understand.

As do you.

That what exists ahead,

is a Beautiful Place.

But in this Life,

to mistreat the moment in the Name of this Notion,

is to miss out on the eternality of it all,

for your responsibility is Here,

not There.

The Stairs

Fours

The Force that desires to

extend your life into the future is the

same Force that keeps you from experiencing

what we know as

Here and Now.

ALL IN ALL

And so now that

we have arrived here,

I suppose I better say that

this book,

these words,

and this life,

are all about trying to

Understand how much we

Don't Understand.

God Bless.

Thank You.

www.ingramcontent.com/pod-product-compliance
Lightning Source LLC
LaVergne TN
LVHW051515070426
835507LV00023B/3117